ADRENALINE RUSH

FREE RUNNING

JACKSON TELLER

A+

Smart Apple Media

Published by Smart Apple Media,
an imprint of Black Rabbit Books
P.O. Box 3263, Mankato, Minnesota 56002
www.blackrabbitbooks.com

Printed in the United States of America at
Corporate Graphics, North Mankato, Minnesota.

Published by arrangement with the
Watts Publishing Group LTD, London.

Library of Congress Cataloging-in-Publication Data

Teller, Jackson.
Free running / Jackson Teller.
p. cm.—(Adrenaline rush)
Includes index.
Summary: "Describes the origins and techniques
of parkour and free running. Describes the
differences between the two activities and
highlights the founders of the sports, along with
how the sport has been highlighted in films and
ads"—Provided by publisher.
ISBN 978-1-59920-682-0 (library binding)
1. Running—Juvenile literature. 2. Parkour—
Juvenile literature. I. Title.
GV1061.T44 2013
796.42—dc23

                              2011053500

Produced by Tall Tree Ltd

PO1433
2-2012

9 8 7 6 5 4 3 2 1

Picture credits:
front cover Sergiy Goruppa/istockphoto.com,
back cover Chris Hepburn/istockphoto.com,
1 Brooke Whatnall/Dreamstime.com, 4 Radin
Myroslav/Shutterstock, 5 Thinkstock Images,
6 geishaboy500/GNU, 7 Tatiana Belova/
Dreamstime.com, 8 Emmanuel Fradin/Reuters/
Corbis, 9 AF archive/Alamy, 10 Sergey Goruppa/
Dreamstime.com, 11t Suprijono Suharjoto/
Dreamstime.com, 11b AF archive/Alamy
12-13 David Spurdens/Corbis, 13 Paul Cowan/
Shutterstock, 14 Arturo Limon/istockphoto,
15 Sergey Goruppa/Dreamstime.com, 16 Olexa/
Shutterstock, 17 Forest Woodward/istockphoto,
18 Olexa/Dreamstime.com, 19 Action Press/Rex
Features, 20 Photosky/Dreamstime.com,
21 Innovatedcaptures/Dreamstime.com, ,
22 Paul Cowan/Shutterstock, 22-23 Brooke
Whatnall/Dreamstime.com, 24-25 Olexa/
Shutterstock, 25 Getty Images, 26-27 Getty
Images, 27 Photos 12/Alamy, 28–29 Tim Clayton/
Corbis, 29 istockphoto

Disclaimer
The website addresses (URLs) included in this
book were valid at the time of going to press.
However, because of the nature of the Internet, it
is possible that some addresses have changed, or
sites may have changed or closed down since
publication. While the author and publisher regret
any inconvenience this may cause to readers, no
responsibility for any such changes can be
accepted either by the author or the publisher.

In preparation of this book, all due care has been
exercised with regard to the advice, activities and
techniques depicted. The publishers regret that
they can accept no liability for any loss or injury
sustained. When learning a new activity, it is
important to get expert advice and to follow a
manufacturer's instructions.

Words in **bold** are in the glossary on page 30.

CONTENTS

Most people live surrounded by concrete and bricks, but we hardly notice the stairs, walls, slopes, parking ramps, and other structures that surround us. In free running or parkour, however, this concrete world is a combination of a gym and a playground.

The walls of a stairwell provide a dramatic backdrop for a stunning free running leap.

Free Runners Everywhere

Today, many of the world's cities and towns have a free running scene. London, New York, Tokyo, Madrid, and Paris are real hotbeds of free running. Every day, new free runners watch online videos to check out the latest moves from around the world and post their own.

Free running is dangerous. Never attempt free running techniques without training and supervision.

Top Three Free Running Movies
- Casino Royale—*this Bond movie opens with one of the most spectacular free running chases ever filmed.*
- Yamakasi *and* Banlieue 13 (*also called* District B13)—*two French movies by the famous director Luc Besson, featuring many of the original free runners.*

The Growth of Free Running

What has made free running so popular?

- Running fast through the urban landscape doing things most other people cannot do is very exciting.

- No one pushes you—there are no coaches shouting instructions and no audience watching.

- Free running requires almost no special equipment.

Free running is about you, your surroundings, and how far you want to push yourself.

Many people record their moves and upload them to websites for others to view and comment on.

Free running grew from a similar activity called parkour. Parkour (called PK for short) was developed in France. A small group of friends in Lisses, a town near Paris, developed many of the skills that free runners now use. What inspired them?

Crocodiles in the Stairwell

Lisses had few places for young people to spend their time. The kids would entertain themselves by setting challenges. Imagining there were crocodiles in the stairwells, for example, they would dare each other to jump safely across. The challenge was to move around without touching the ground, by leaping from wall to bench to pole to tree. The skills they developed turned into **parkour**.

A free runner launches into a move from a wall. Free running combines flexibility, agility, and strength to create breath-taking moves.

Handrails, stairs, walls, and other street fixtures give free runners a chance to practice their skills.

- *Parkour is a respelling of the French word parcours, which describes a route or a distance covered.*
- *People who take part in parkour are called traceurs. This French word describes something that leaves a trail behind it. In Paris, where parkour developed, "tracer" is slang for hurrying or moving quickly.*

Fighting Fires

One of the founders of parkour, David Belle, was from a family of firefighters. Both his father and grandfather had made many daring rescues from burning buildings. Belle hoped that one day parkour skills could be used to make similar rescues in dangerous situations. Based off of this, the emphasis in parkour is getting from one place to another as quickly as possible.

Among the first traceurs were David Belle and Sébastien Foucan. Belle is said to be the founder of parkour. Most people view Foucan as the creator of free running.

David Belle and Parkour

David Belle was originally from northern France, and moved to Lisses when he was 15. As a teenager he was good at gymnastics, climbing, track, and martial arts.

Belle combined these skills into one method for moving around the city. This became known as parkour. Parkour uses leaps, **twists**, and **flips**—but only if they help the traceur to move forward.

Parkour traceurs, such as David Belle (pictured here), believe that any technique that uses unnecessary time or energy is a waste.

Sébastien Foucan and Free Running

Sébastien Foucan helped fellow Frenchman David Belle develop parkour, but for Foucan, moving around efficiently wasn't enough. He wanted to do something that was also spectacular to look at. He added spins, twists, and other tricks to his moves. Foucan's version of parkour became known as free running.

Sébastien Foucan's free running skills soon attracted the attention of TV and film producers.

Belle on Screen
Like many famous traceurs, David Belle has appeared in may genres of entertainment, including:
- *Films, such as Banlieue 13 and Banlieue 13 Ultimatum, Transporter 2 and Prince of Persia.*
- *Many ads, among them one for the BBC in 2002.*

One of the best things about free running is that it does not require much equipment. In fact, most people already have what they need in the closet at home. This means anyone can start free running for practically no cost.

Running shoes have to fit really well, and be laced tightly enough to stay on if they get caught on something. Free runners prefer shoes with some shock absorption in the soles in order to cushion landings.

Loose shorts or pants and T-shirts give free runners enough freedom to perform moves easily.

Free running is really hard work. Free runners sweat a lot, so they need to drink water regularly. A dehydrated traceur risks losing strength, coordination, and balance—which could be disastrous.

Extra Gear

Some free runners do spend additional money on equipment:

- Soft gloves protect hands when doing tricks. The gloves need to be soft enough so they do not affect grip.

- A few free runners wear **body armor**. Others feel that armor gets in the way, or tempts them to try things they are not actually capable of doing.

France's Cyril Raffaelli was one of the first traceurs. Born in 1974, he is a year younger than David Belle. He joined a circus school at age 14 to train as an **acrobat**, and later got a job with the Fratellini Circus. Raffaelli is also an expert in the Japanese martial art karate. He now works as a movie stuntman and body double, and has appeared in movies alongside his friend Belle many times.

CYRIL RAFFAELLI

In 2003, a documentary called *Jump London* appeared. It was Sébastien Foucan's first chance to show his new form of parkour to the world. The one-hour film was so breathtaking that it inspired many to try free running.

The skyline of London, including St Paul's Cathedral, provided the backdrop to the breathtaking moves of Jump London.

The Runners

As well as Sébastien Foucan, *Jump London* featured two other free runners:

- Jerome Ben Aoues—he first met Foucan not long after free running had begun to develop. Ben Aoues often works on the same movies, ads, and demonstrations as Foucan.

- Johann Vigroux —he learned free running from the original Lisses runners. He later took part in the 2009 film *Parkour in America*, which showed free running to a whole new audience.

London Locations

Jump London featured some of the most famous locations in London. Getting permission to run and film at these places was tricky, but the runners visited:

- Shakespeare's Globe Theatre
- The Royal Albert Hall
- The Tate Modern art gallery
- The narrow streets of Soho

The film finished with Foucan performing an amazing leap from an upper deck of HMS *Belfast*.

The release of Jump London led to an incredible growth of free running throughout the United Kingdom, as shown by these two traceurs performing in the seaside town of Great Yarmouth.

Free Running on TV
After Jump London, *there have been many more TV shows about free running. They include:*

- *In 2009 and 2010, the series Ultimate Parkour Challenge featured some the best free runners in the world. They included Danny Arroyo, King David, Daniel Ilabaca, and Oleg Vorslav.*
- *In 2011, Jump City: Seattle appeared. It pitted four teams of top free runners against each other in the streets of Seattle, Washington.*

It is one thing to think to yourself, "I could do that." It is another to actually get up and do it. Free running is a demanding activity and potentially dangerous. So, how do free runners get started?

First Steps

You need to be fit to do free running, and **gymnastics** experience will help a lot. Many free runners begin their training using this three-point plan.

• Picking a place in the distance, a free runner will try using different routes to get there.

• Once a route has been chosen, the free runner will try that route, traveling slowly at first.

• The free runner will then gradually add speed and harder skills.

Free runners start off by practicing moves on low objects such as a park bench.

Training as a Group

Many people find free running easier to learn and more rewarding in a small group. The members of the group encourage each other—though never so much that inexperienced runners feel pressured into trying things they cannot do.

Different free runners are good at different skills, so they can teach one another new techniques. A group might even hire a free running coach who can teach them completely new tricks.

Three free runners guide each other down the side of a building, using the stair railings on each level.

Top Three Free Running Characters
Lots of computer games feature characters with free running skills. Three of the best are:
- *The Prince in the* Prince of Persia *games (so good they were made into a movie!).*
- *The gang of outlaws in* Mirror's Edge.
- *Altair ibn La-Ahad and Ezio Auditore da Firenze in* Assassin's Creed.

ON THE SCREEN

Free runners work to move quickly and smoothly through the urban environment—just like an animal. So it is no wonder that animals have inspired some of their techniques. Monkey vaults and cat balances are basic free running techniques. Watch any free running sequence and you will probably see them performed.

This runner is mid-air during a monkey vault.

The Monkey Vault

Free runners use the monkey vault to jump obstacles such as low walls or handrails. But how do the runners do it?

• The runner heads toward the obstacle and jumps forward off both feet from about 5 feet (1.5 m) away.

• The arms swing forward and extend, and the hands land together on the obstacle.

• The runner tucks the legs up under the body and lets them swing through, then pushes off with the hands.

This is a nice, smooth move, and the runner will try to land easily and keep running.

Cat Balances

Free runners use cat balances to move along obstacles such as walls and handrails. They learn the technique on a wide, low wall, but the best free runners use the cat balance on walls and rails high above the ground. Both hands and feet are used on the obstacle, and the runner scampers along it like a cat. The runner keeps his or her body low, as this is the key to a successful cat balance.

During a cat balance, the free runner keeps one hand and one foot in contact at all times.

Basic Moves
These are some of the basic moves of parkour and free running:
- *Roll—forward roll used as a **breakfall**, to absorb some of the impact when landing from jumps.*
- *Precision—jump from one obstacle to land onto a precise spot somewhere else.*
- *Turn vault/turn down—vault or drop in which the runner turns halfway around, often used to hang from something before dropping down.*

Running up a wall—how cool is that? The wall run is a technique that looks easy until you stop and think about what is involved. This trick is also called the pop vault, wall pass, and wall hop. Whatever you call it, this is the move all new free runners want to learn as soon as possible.

Use of the Wall Run

Free runners can use the wall run to get over a wall taller than their own heads. They can dodge a flight of stairs or avoid a long detour simply by running up a wall that is in their way.

*Instead of running up the wall, this free runner has added a **flair** to create an impressive move.*

Effortless Skill

A successful wall run requires smoothness and speed. Good free runners make this difficult skill look easy.

This free runner is practicing a wall run at a training session at Stuttgart University in Germany.

- The runner approaches the wall at a comfortable speed, then leaps up and plants the front of the foot on the wall, just above hip height.

- With the front foot planted firmly on the wall, the runner pushes off and up. Using the arms to drive the body up, the runner reaches the top of the wall with the hands. The runner can now pull up, swing a leg onto the top, and keep running.

Highest Wall Run
In January 2009, Link Demarco of Spain set a new world record for the highest wall run ever. He ran up a wall that was 11.8 ft (3.6 m) high—too high for most elephants to look over.

KNOW THE FACTS

Many basic parkour moves are also used in free running. But the essence of free running is to add in more difficult, spectacular leaps. Adding these flairs to a run is called **tricking**.

Websters and other flips are used on flat ground or to provide a stunning way of getting down a staircase or a slope.

Head over Heels

The Webster is a front somersault with a one-footed takeoff. The runner takes off on one foot, kicks the trailing leg up in the air behind and uses that motion to do a somersault and keep running. Runners sometimes combine a Webster with other tricks to make it even more spectacular.

This free runner's forearms have uncrossed themselves at the top of a reverse palm spin. By the time he lands it, they will have crossed back.

Reverse Palm Spins

In a reverse palm spring, the runner approaches an obstacle, such as a park bench, with crossed forearms. The runner plants the hands on the bench and spins around them in the air, so that once the spin is complete, the forearms are crossed the opposite way. The runner then pushes off the obstacle and keeps running.

Pizza or Free Running?
"I had two choices: I could sit at home and eat pizza in front of the computer all day, or I could train. I chose to train."

Cyril Raffaelli, martial artist, free runner, and stuntman, who has worked on Die Hard 4, and Transporter 2.

Some flairs are practically guaranteed to draw gasps from onlookers, especially if the audience has not seen free running before. The side flip and the standing full are two of these really spectacular tricks that will wow anyone watching.

Side Flips

The side flip is basically a sideways somersault, often from off the end of a low wall or a flight of steps.

The runner takes off sideways, bouncing up into the air sideways. Once high enough, the runner curls up and does a sideways somersault in the air before landing smoothly and running on.

Side flips provide an interesting way of getting over low objects, such as this wall.

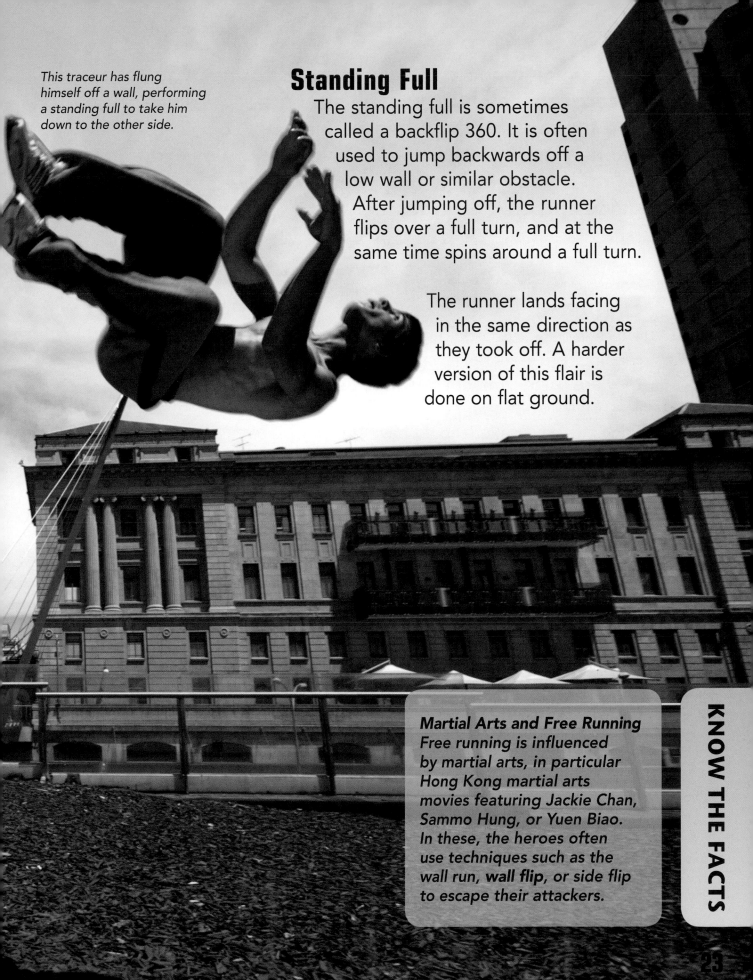

This traceur has flung himself off a wall, performing a standing full to take him down to the other side.

Standing Full

The standing full is sometimes called a backflip 360. It is often used to jump backwards off a low wall or similar obstacle. After jumping off, the runner flips over a full turn, and at the same time spins around a full turn.

The runner lands facing in the same direction as they took off. A harder version of this flair is done on flat ground.

Martial Arts and Free Running
Free running is influenced by martial arts, in particular Hong Kong martial arts movies featuring Jackie Chan, Sammo Hung, or Yuen Biao. In these, the heroes often use techniques such as the wall run, wall flip, or side flip to escape their attackers.

Free running and parkour are good forms of excercise. They build muscle strength, coordination, and fitness. However, free running is also dangerous, with the risk of serious injury or even death if you get it wrong. Traceurs have a few guidelines to make their activity as safe as possible.

Equipment

There is very little equipment in free running, but traceurs always make sure they are using the right gear (see pages 10–11). It needs to be in good condition. Shoes, for example, should have no frayed laces or loose soles.

Falling and Fitness

A key skill for free runners is how to fall. Rather than slamming into the ground, they learn to use forward rolls to absorb the energy of a landing. If they do fall, it is best to relax, rather than tense up, as this makes injury less likely. Traceurs must also keep very fit—accidents and mistakes are much more likely when a runner is out of shape.

In this sequence, the traceur performs a forward roll to absorb the shock of a monkey vault from a high wall.

Attitude

Many traceurs think that free running requires a good mental attitude. Fear causes you to tense up and this will affect performance. A free runner needs to feel confident before attempting a technique.

• If you fail at something, get up, dust yourself off, and try again.

• Be patient, and do not expect to perform big techniques all at once. Practice slowly and on small obstacles at first.

• Never be pushed into trying something you are scared to do or do not think is possible.

Warming up is important in order to avoid injuries. These free runners are stretching before their performance at the unveiling of the Olympic rings in London in 2011.

Free Running Quotes
These quotes all come from parkour and free running websites:
"Whether you think you can or think you can't, you are right."
"In order to succeed, you must fail, so that you know what not to do the next time."
"Courage doesn't always roar. Sometimes courage is the quiet voice at the end of the day saying, 'I will try again tomorrow.'"
"Fear is the highest wall."

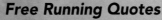

KNOW THE FACTS

Advertisers and moviemakers were quick to realize that free running would look great on screen. Today, one of the main ways for free runners to make money is by appearing in movies, TV shows, and ads.

Movies

Free running has now appeared in hundreds of movies. Probably the most famous is *Casino Royale*, in which James Bond pursues Sébastien Foucan through a construction site. Free running also appeared in the next Bond movie, *Quantum of Solace*, and in the third Bourne film, *The Bourne Ultimatum*. In *Prince of Persia*, 13-year-old English free runner Will Foster shows off his skills while being chased through a marketplace.

Traceurs for the 3Run display team perform at the world premiere of Prince of Persia.

Sébastien Foucan in action (above) during the Bond movie Casino Royale.

Music

Madonna did a lot to spread free running's popularity when she used it extensively in her videos for "Jump" and "Hung Up." Her "Confessions" tour also used free running techniques in the **choreography**. Bands such as 3 Doors Down and Bon Jovi as well as the Swedish DJ Eric Prydz have also used free running in their videos.

Top Two Free Running Ads
- *David Belle's appearance as a free runner beating the rush hour traffic is a classic.*
- *Sébastien Foucan being chased by an angry chicken.*

Find both of these ads at www.americanparkour.com

If you could jump in your private jet and fly off anywhere in the world, where would you pick to go free running? These free running hotspots would have to make it onto your shortlist!

Members of the Voltz Parkour team practise off a wall in Rio de Janeiro, Brazil.

Lisses, France

All the obstacles that Belle and Foucan used to develop their original parkour and free running moves are still there. These include:

- The emergency staircase known as L'Escaliers, which often appears in films.
- The Parc du Lac—the sculpture known as the Dame du Lac is where the first traceurs started out.

San Francisco and Seattle

Both these West Coast cities have big free running communities. There are regular training and demonstration sessions, often organized online. Check out www.sfparkour.com and www.seattleparkour.com for more information.

Rio de Janeiro, Brazil

Rio is one of the world's biggest and busiest cities. It is no surprise that people escape the congestion by going free running!

Australia

There are active parkour and free running groups in most big cities, including Adelaide, Brisbane, Canberra, Melbourne, Perth, and Sydney. The best place to start looking for information is www.parkour.asn.au—the home page has links to the details of various classes.

London, United Kingdom

You will not be able to run the same buildings as in *Jump London*, but the UK's largest city still has plenty to offer free runners. The best spots include Vauxhall Walls, The Fortress, Elephant and Castle, Waterloo, and Embankment.

A free runner launches himself from building to building in a suburban housing estate near Paris.

acrobat
person who performs spectacular gymnastic moves.

body armor
hard plastic plates, usually sewn to a tight-fitting T-shirt or shorts, which are worn for protection.

body double
person who takes the place of a star actor in a movie because something dangerous or embarrassing is being filmed.

breakfall
technique for absorbing some of the force of a landing, used in free running and martial arts.

choreography
combination of movement and music; a planned dance or movement that goes with a piece of music.

flair
free running technique with extra difficulty added to make it more spectacular.

flips
techniques involving the body turning end over end through 360 degrees or more.

gymnastics
a sport that involves training in strength and agility, which develops a lot of the skills needed for free running.

parkour
earliest form of free running, in which the emphasis is on moving as fast and efficiently as possible.

tricking
performing flairs while free running.

twists
spins on a vertical axis.

wall flip
technique in which the free runner runs at a wall, jumps up to place one foot against it, then pushes off into a backward flip.

Organizations

American Parkour

Focusing on keeping the parkour and free running communities local, American Parkour built a network of affiliates in many states. These organizations offer training, advice, demonstrations, and chances to connect with other traceurs. Find them at www.americanparkour.com.

Parkour.com

Sébastien Foucan founded this website as a way to keep traceurs connected and informed. Find articles, photos, and videos at www.parkour.com.

Urban Freeflow

In the United Kingdom, Urban Freeflow describes itself as the "Official Worldwide Parkour and Free Running Network." As well as organizing various competitions, it has a team of free runners and some excellent tutorial videos on the website at www.urbanfreeflow.com.

Competitions

Many traceurs feel that personal improvement, rather than competition is the spirit of their activity. However, the Urban Freeflow group runs an online "World Championship" event. Competitors submit a short, unedited video of themselves in action. The videos are scored based on four key criteria:

- Technical difficulty
- Execution (how cleanly the runners perform techniques)
- Creativity (how imaginatively the runners use the space available to them)
- Fluidity of the transitions between techniques

9/12